# The Plymouth Thanksgiving

written and illustrated

by

Leonard Weisgard

DOUBLEDAY

NEW YORK   LONDON   TORONTO   SYDNEY   AUCKLAND

## PASSENGERS ON THE MAYFLOWER

John Carver, his wife Katherine Carver, Desire Minter,
2 servants John Howland and Roger Wilder,
a boy William Latham, a maid servant, and a child Jasper More.

William Brewster, his wife Mary Brewster,
2 sons Love and Wrestling
and a boy Richard More and his brother.

Edward Winslow, his wife Elizabeth Winslow,
2 servants George Soule and Elias Story,
a little girl Ellen, sister of Richard More.

William Bradford and his wife Dorothy.

Isaac Allerton, his wife Mary Allerton,
their children Bartholomew, Remember and Mary,
a servant boy, John Hooke.

Samuel Fuller, and a servant William Butten.

John Crakston and his son John Crakston.

Captain Myles Standish and his wife Rose.

Christopher Martin, his wife,
2 servants Solomon Prower and John Langmore.

William Mullins, his wife Alice, 2 children Joseph and Priscilla,
a servant Robert Carter.

William White, his wife Susanna, a son Resolved
and one son born on the Mayflower called Peregrine,
2 servants William Holbeck, Edward Thomson.